KAWAII MONSTERS

COLORING BOOK

CUTE COLORING BOOKS FOR ADULT

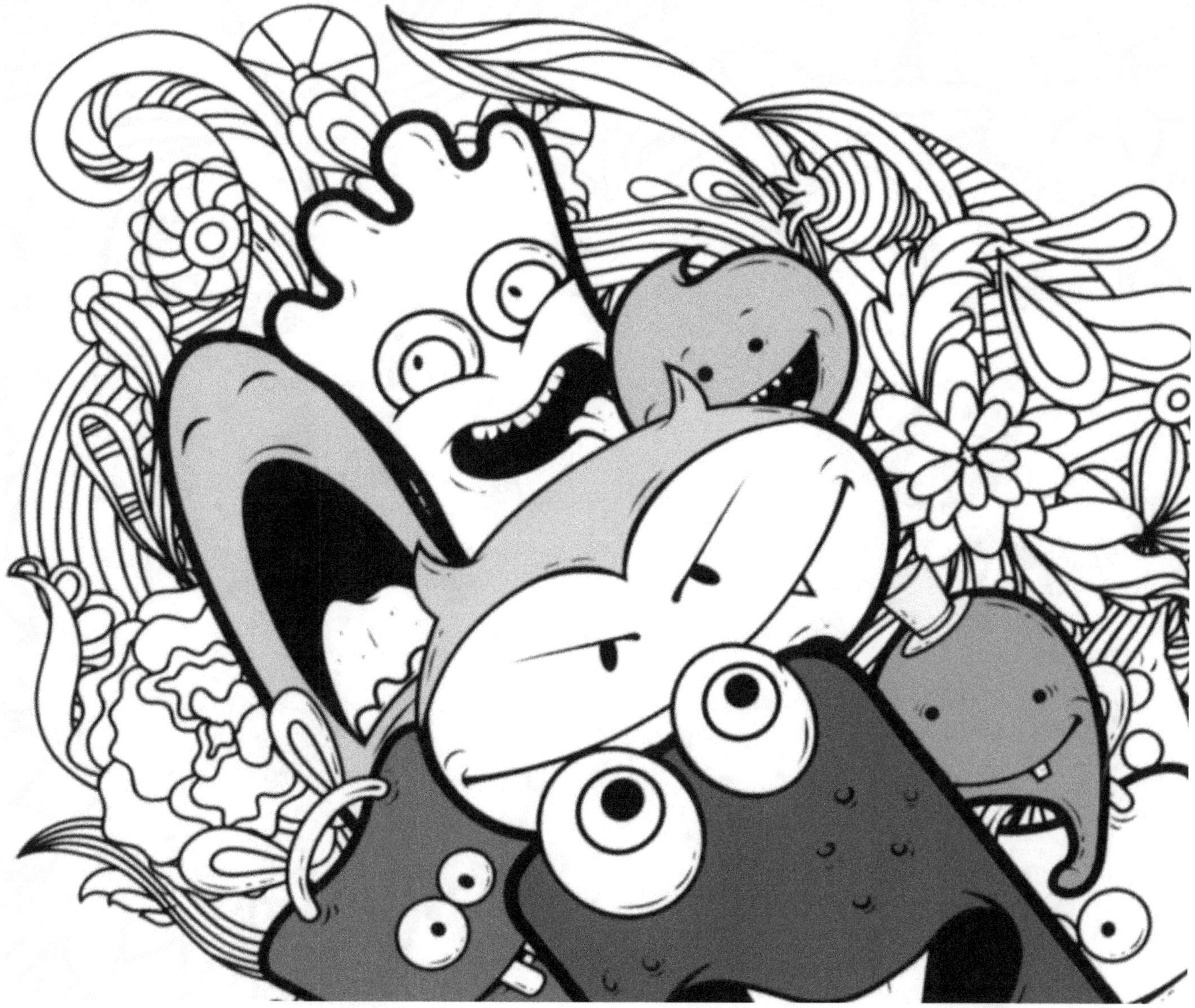

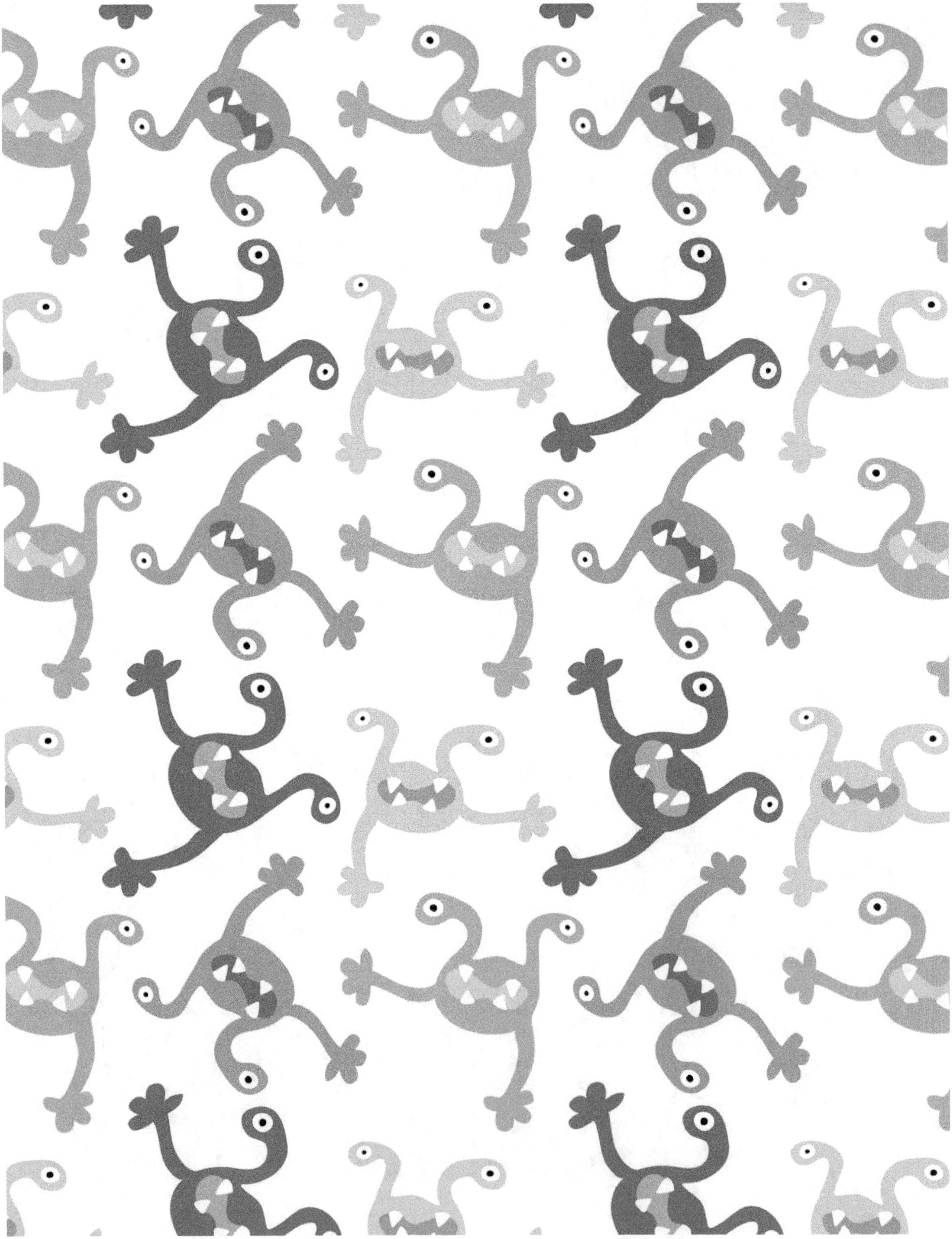

COLOR TEST PAGE

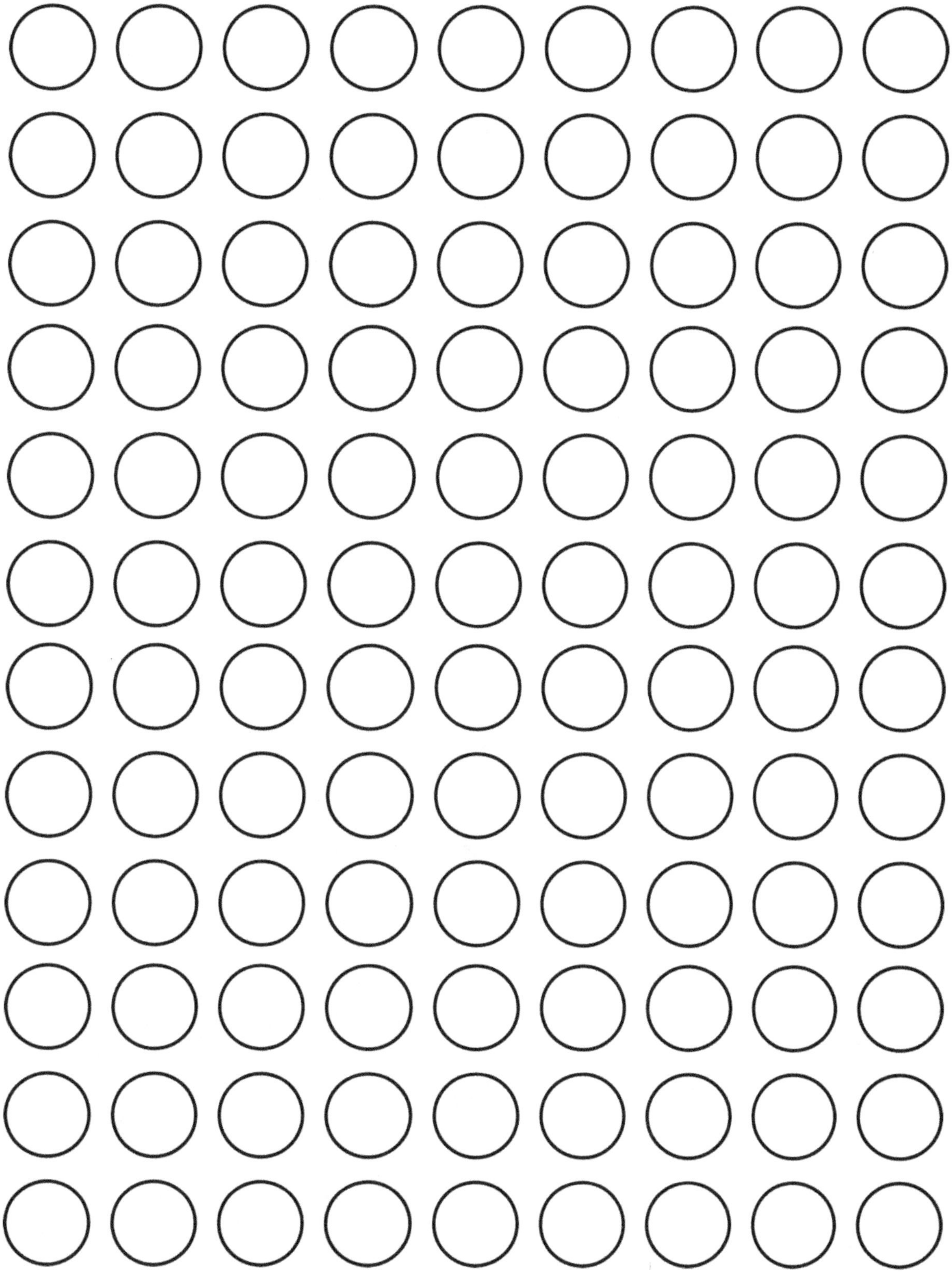

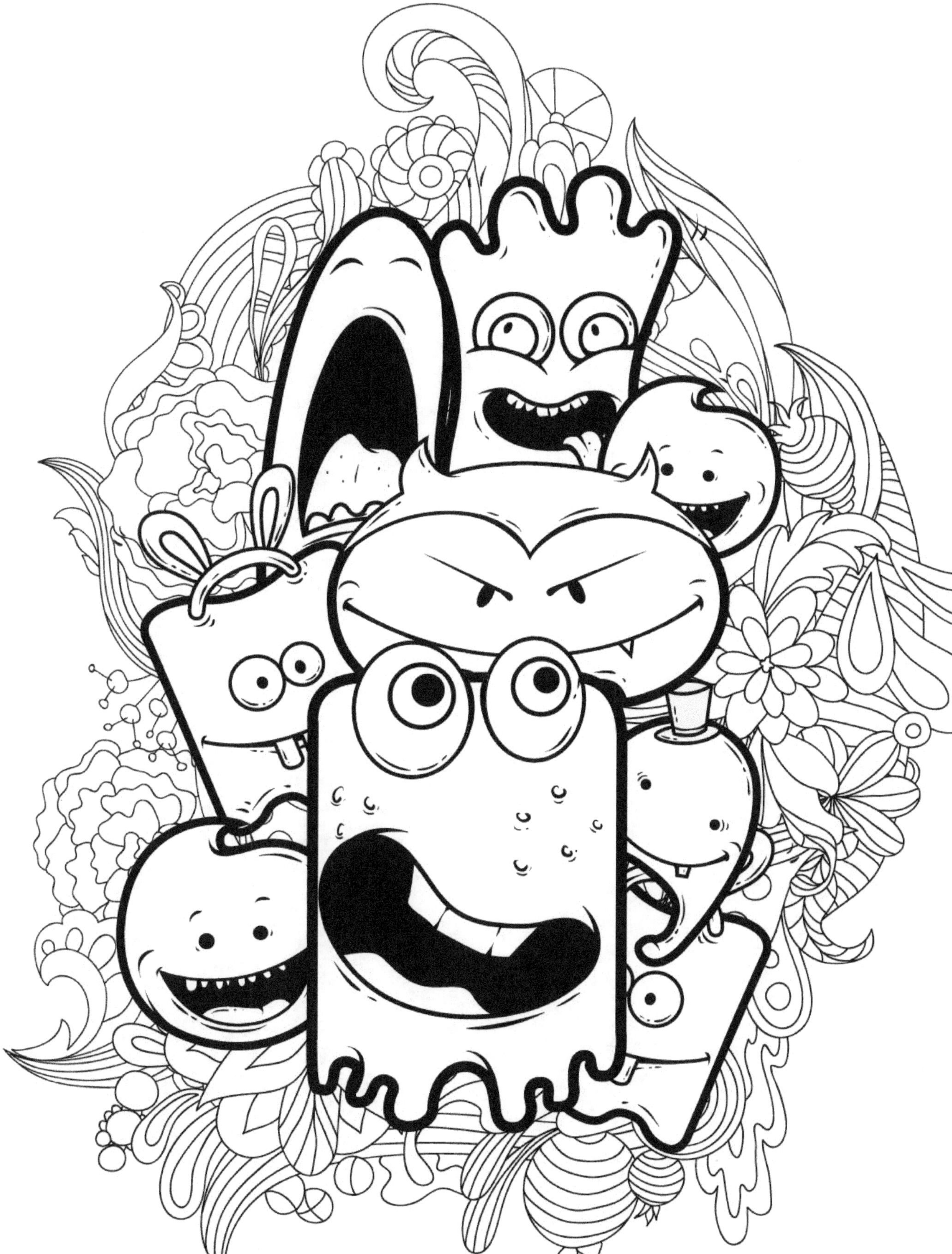

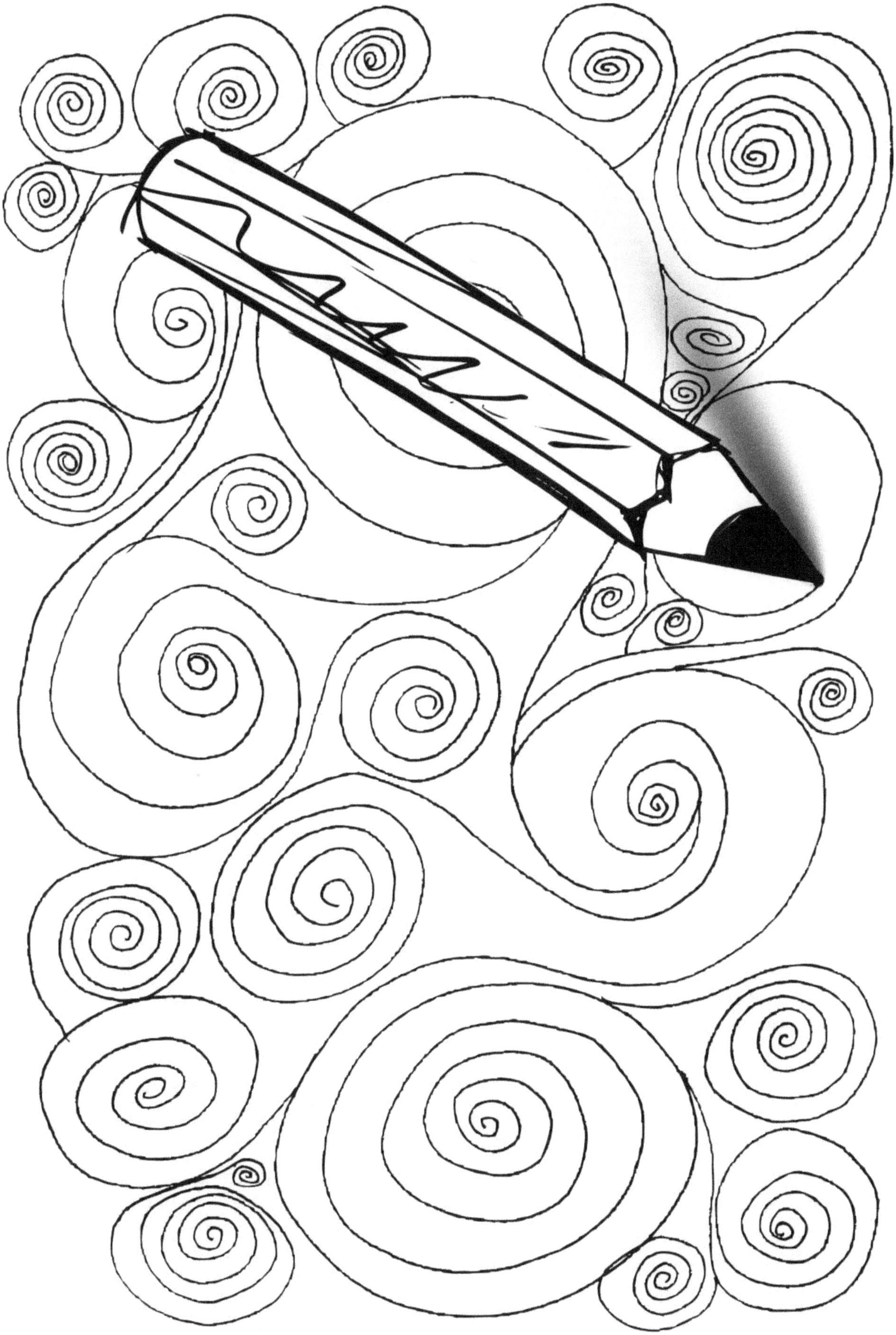

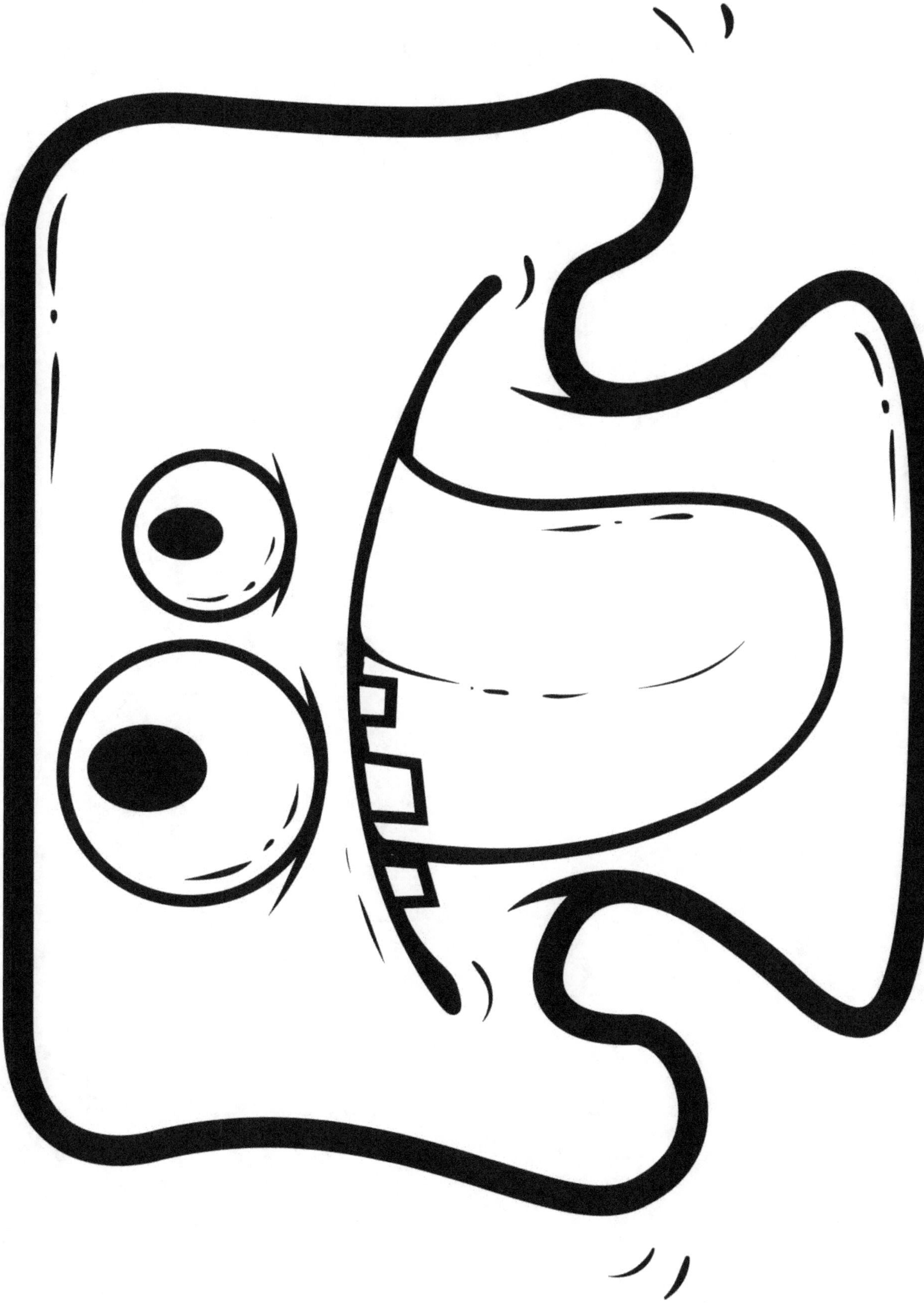

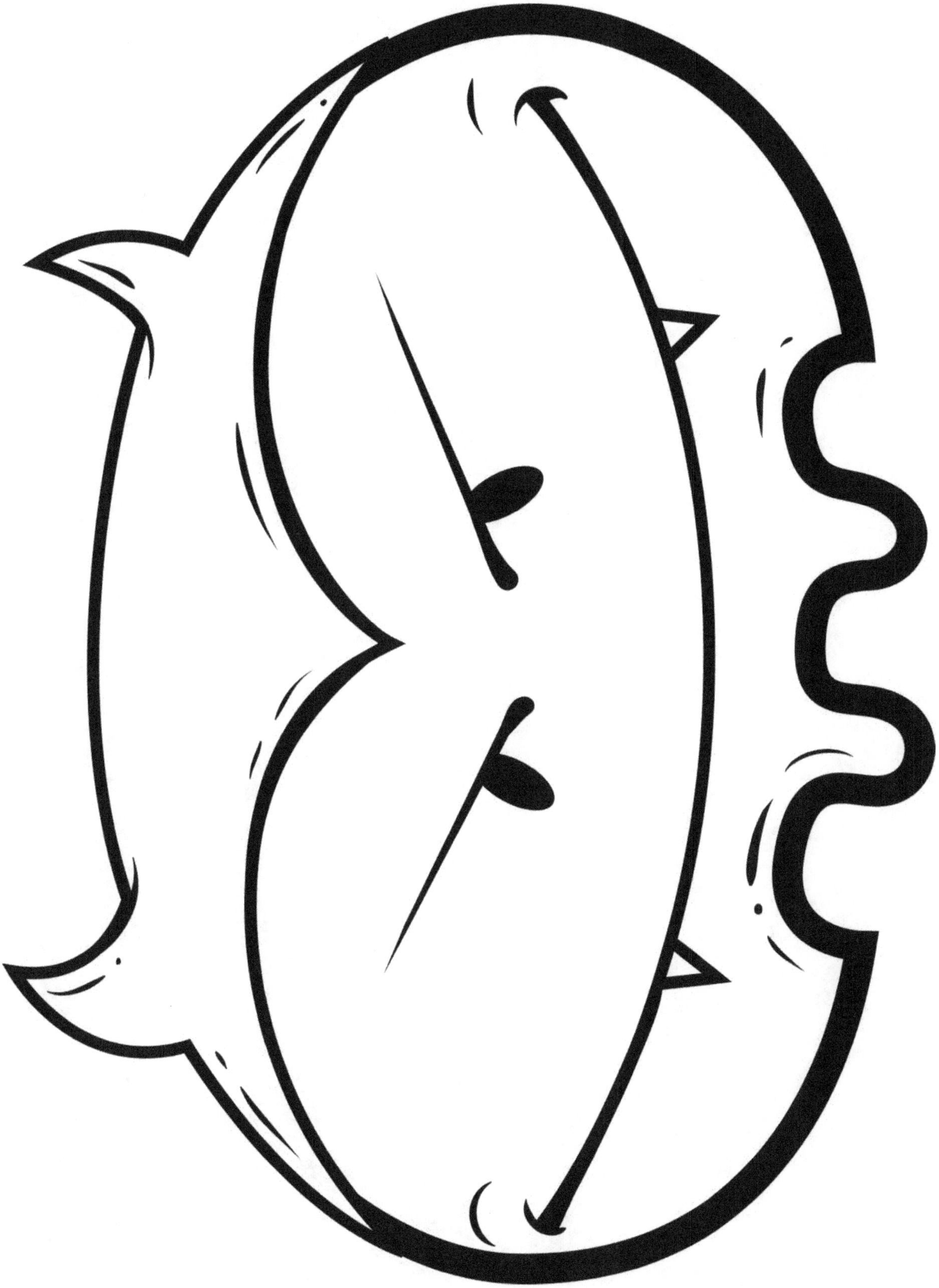

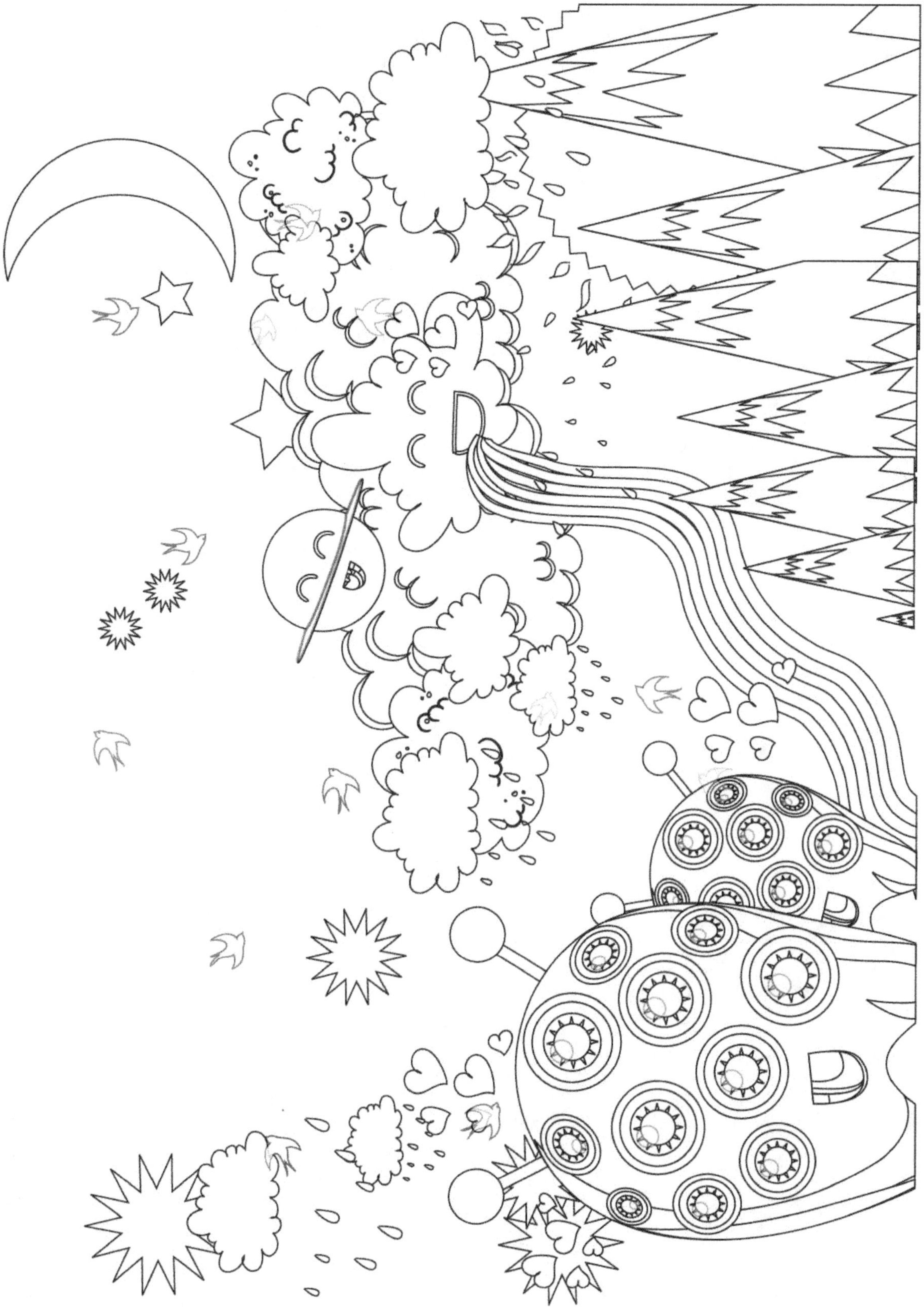

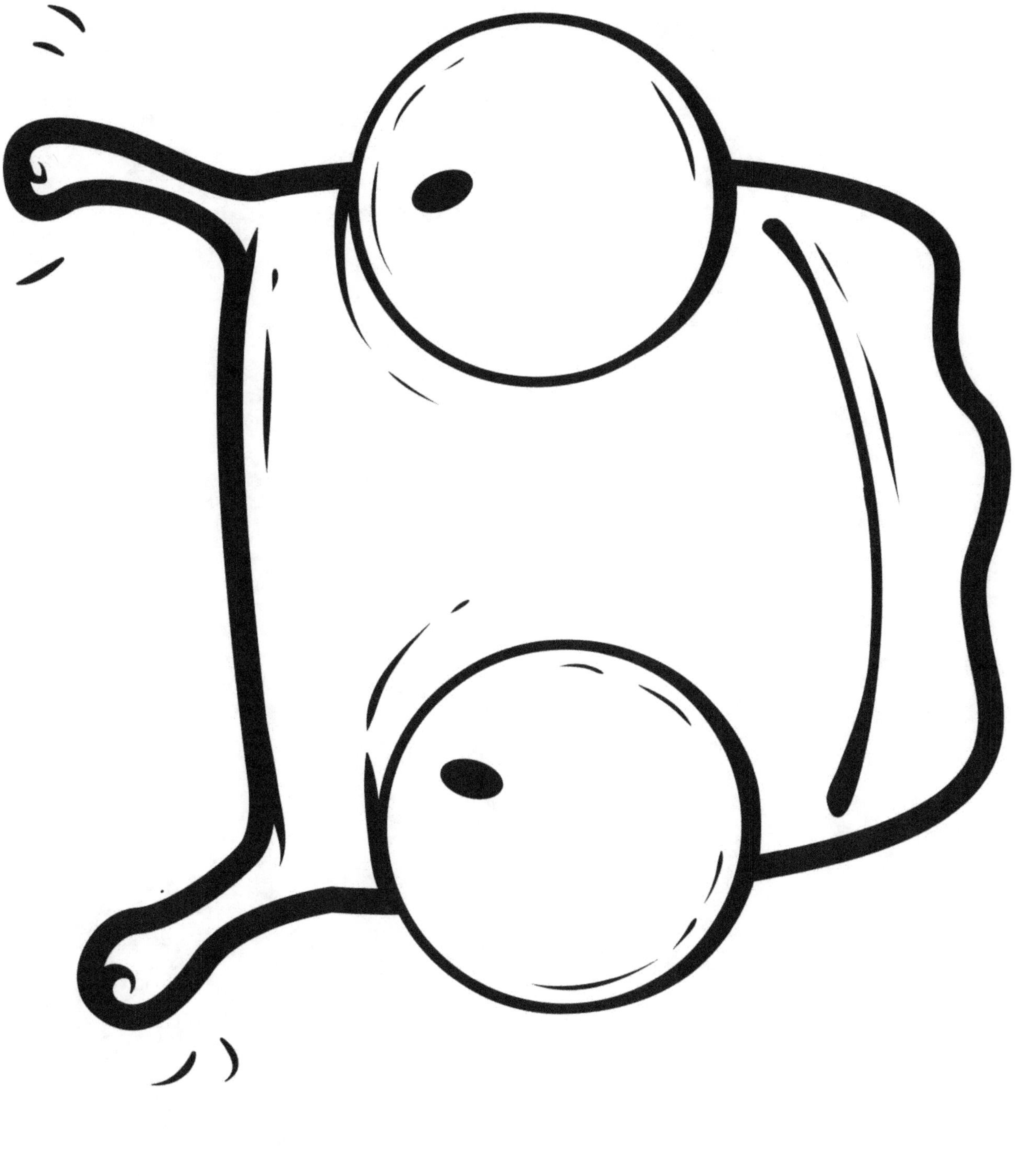

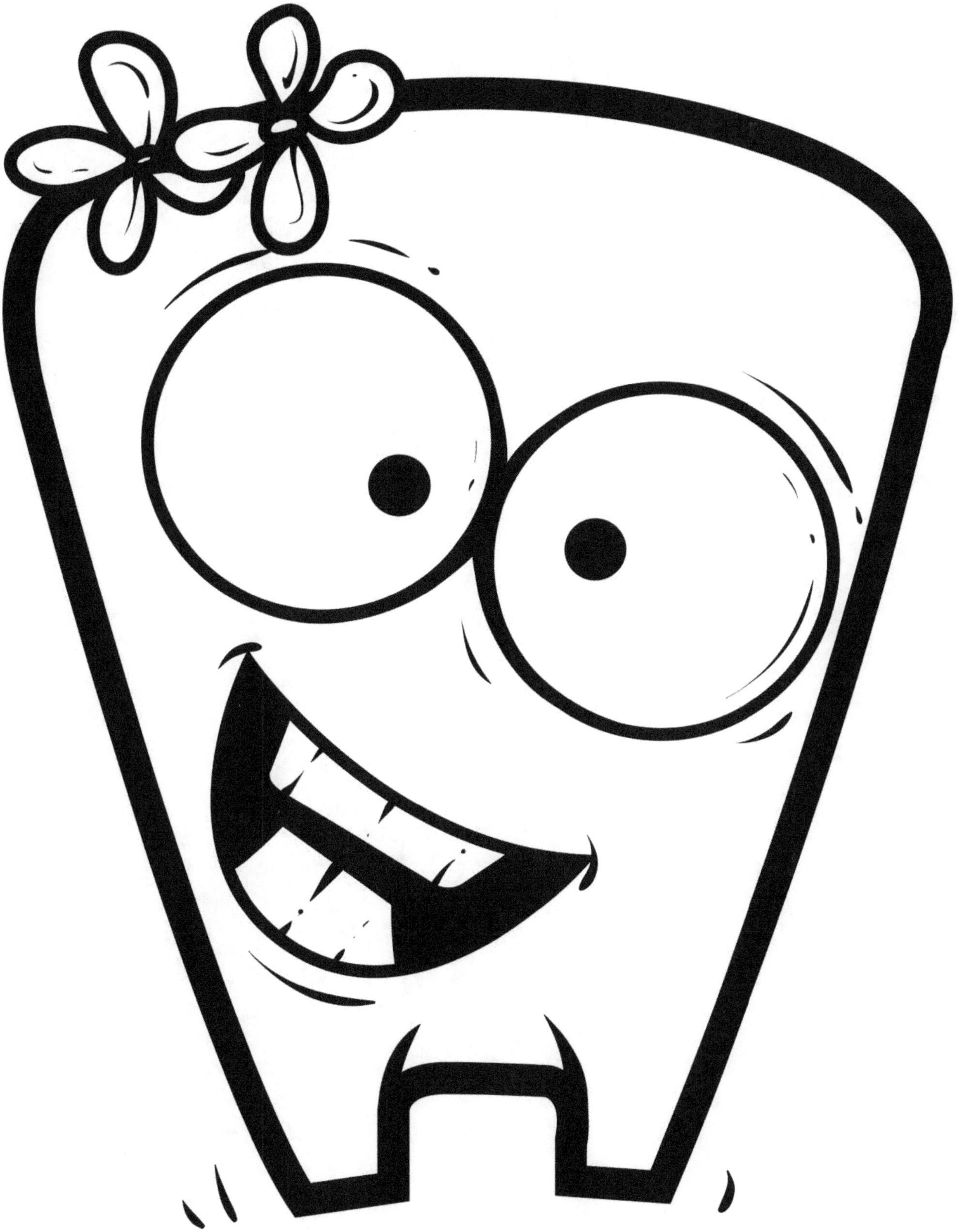

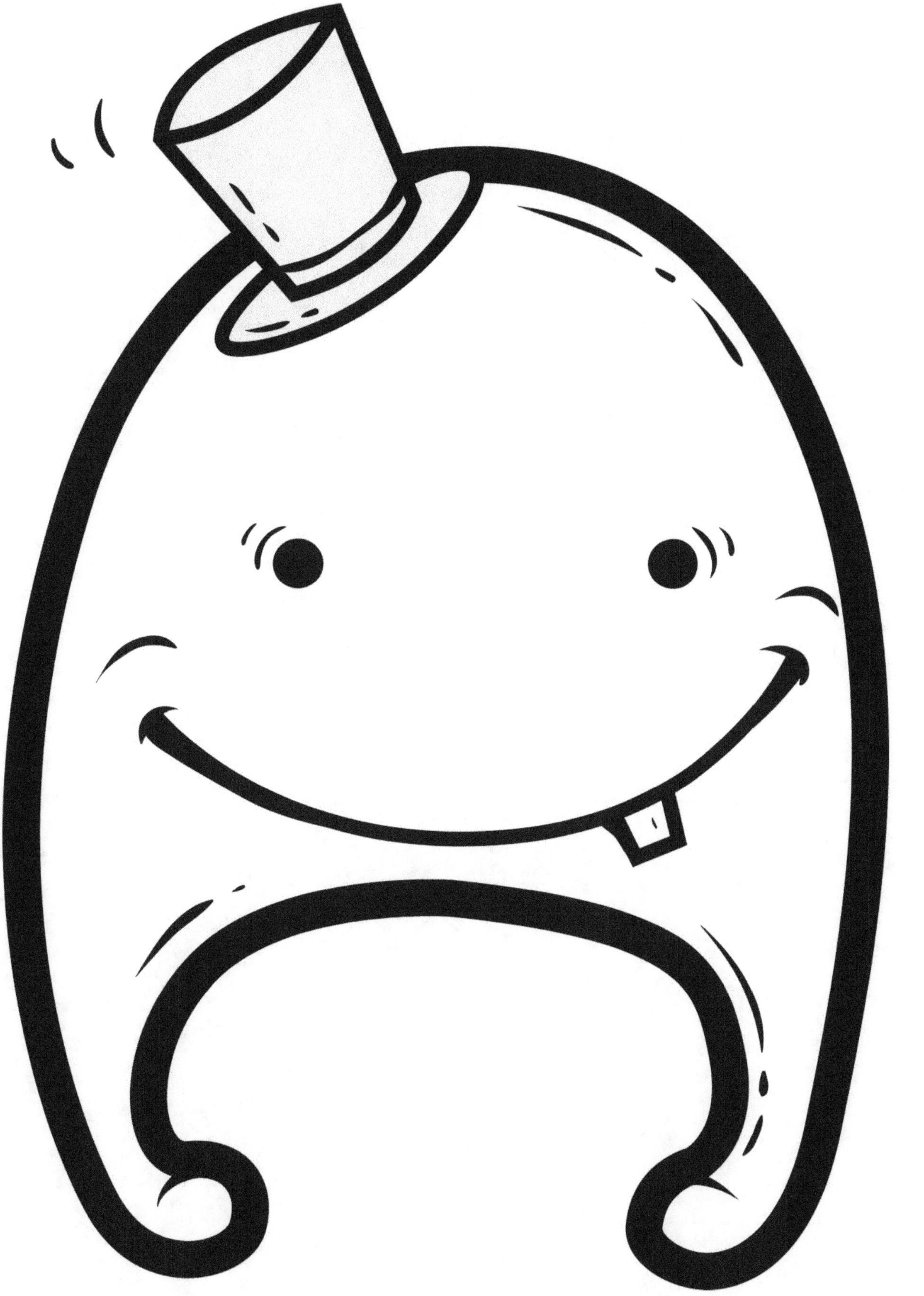

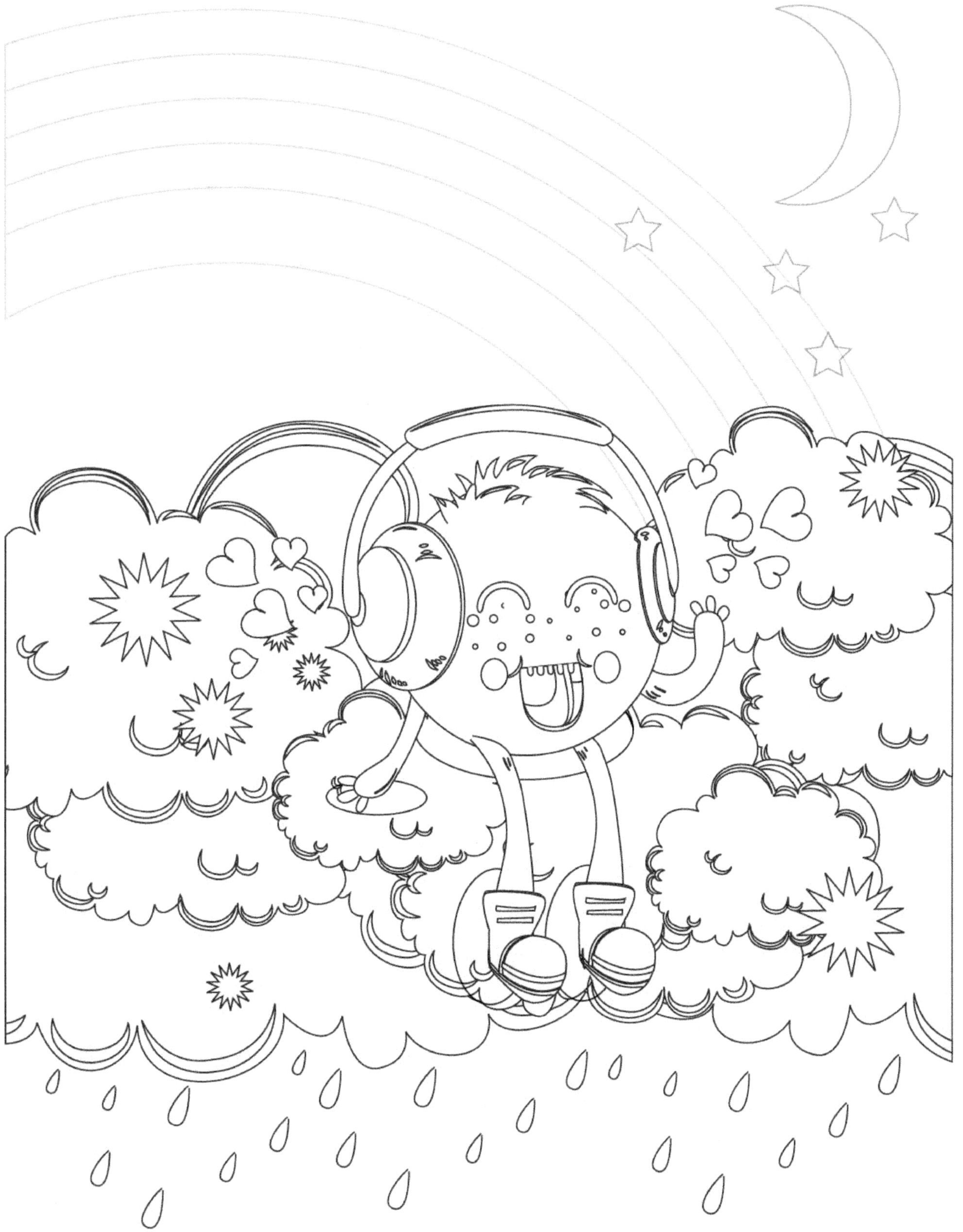

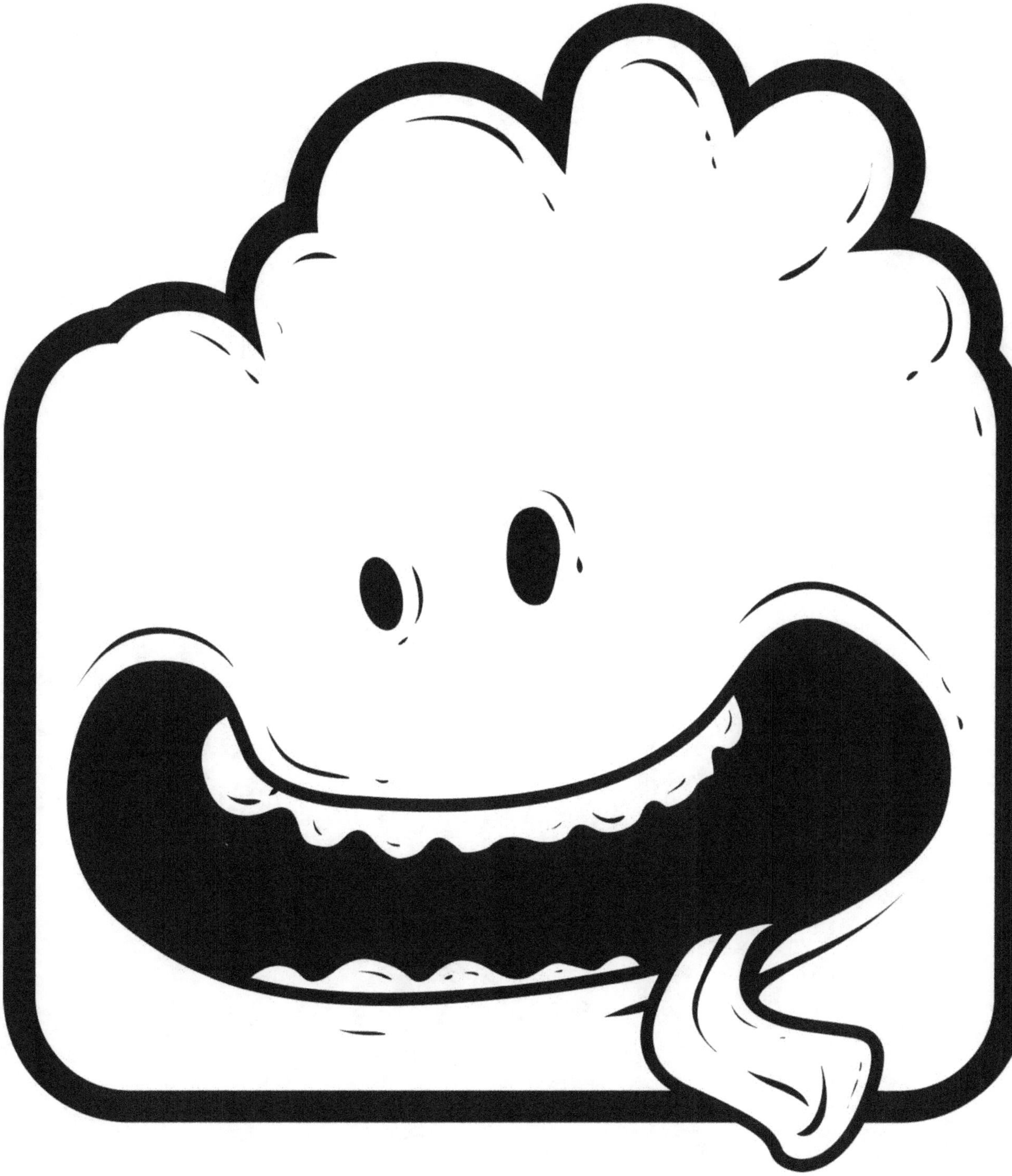

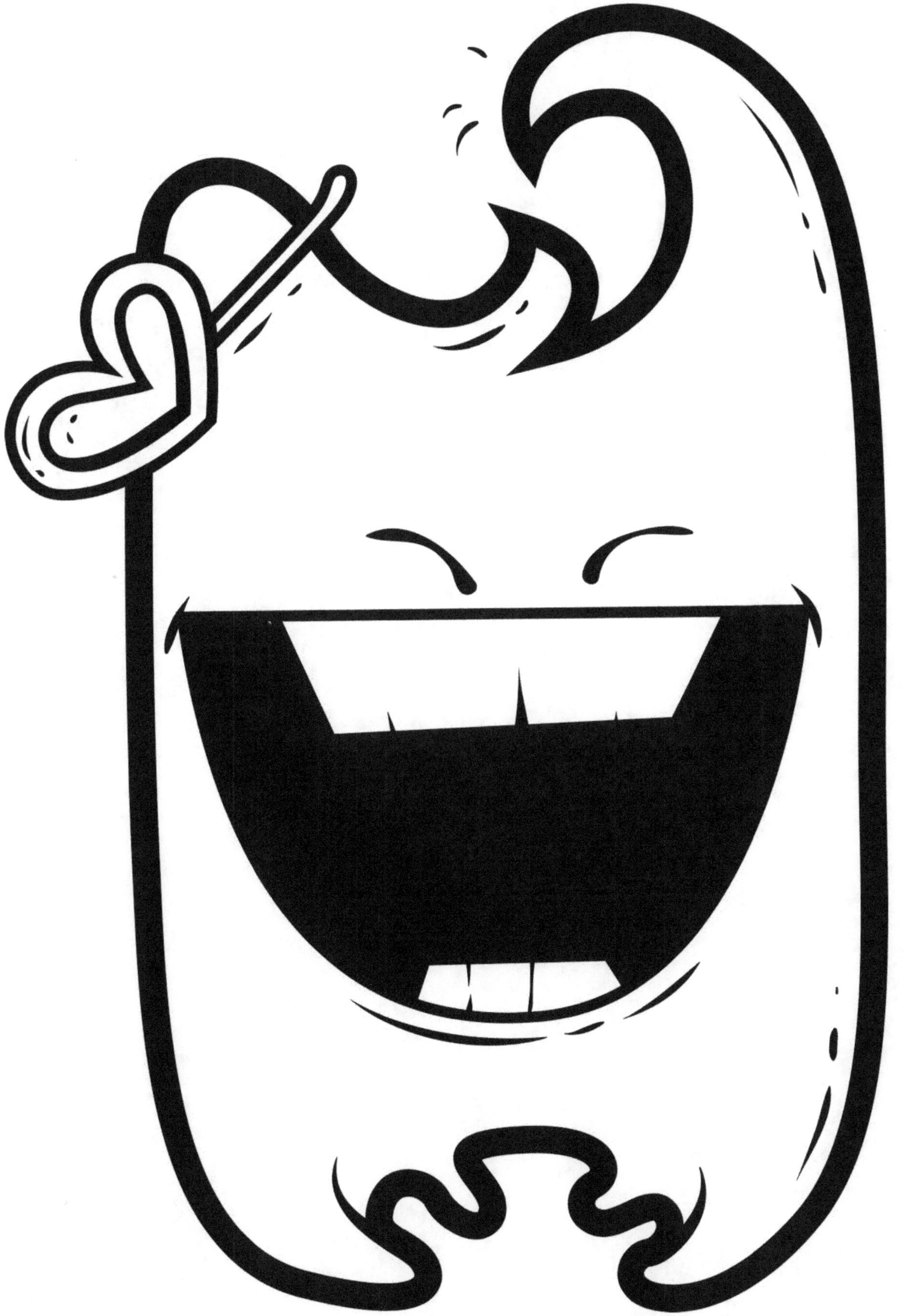

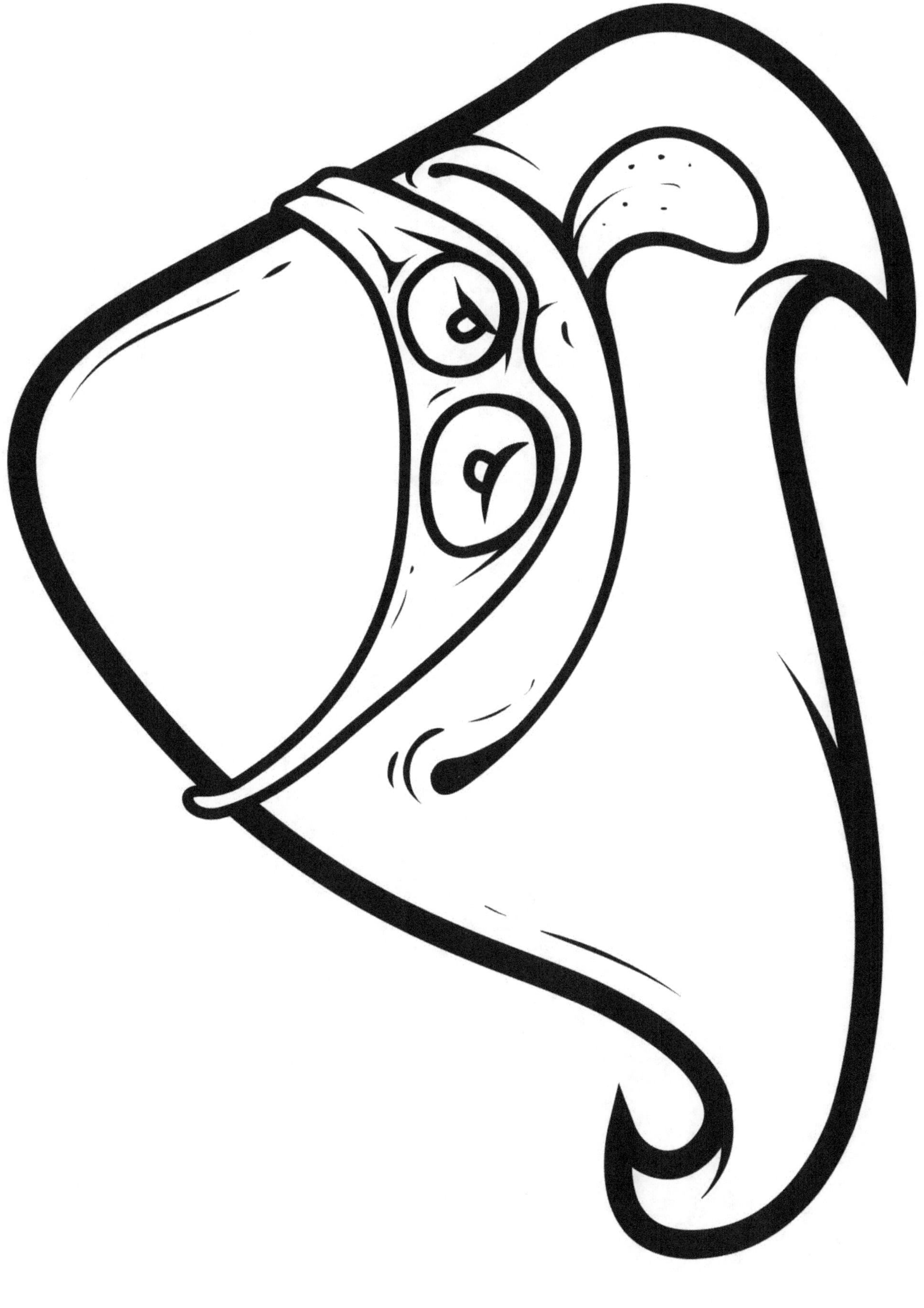

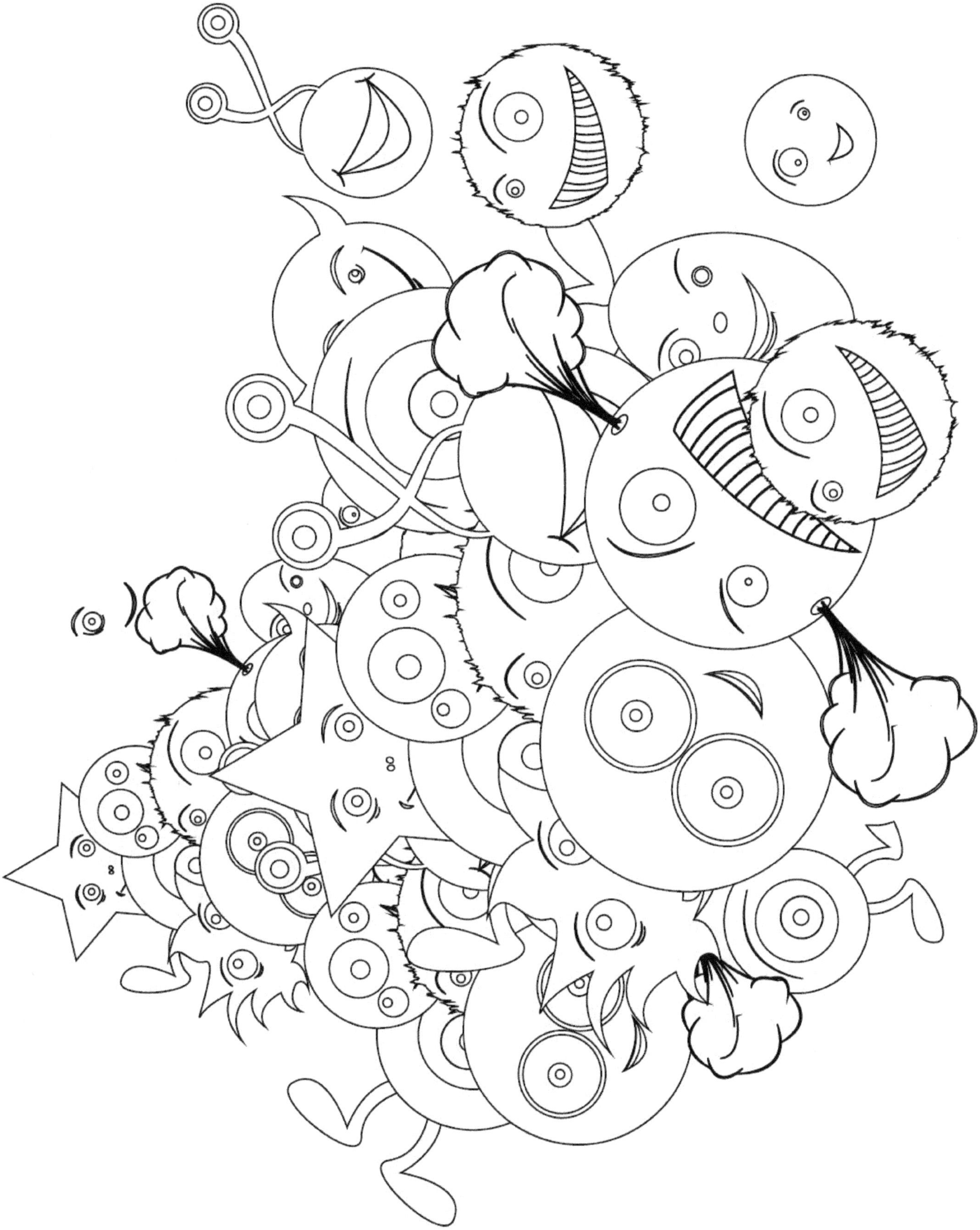

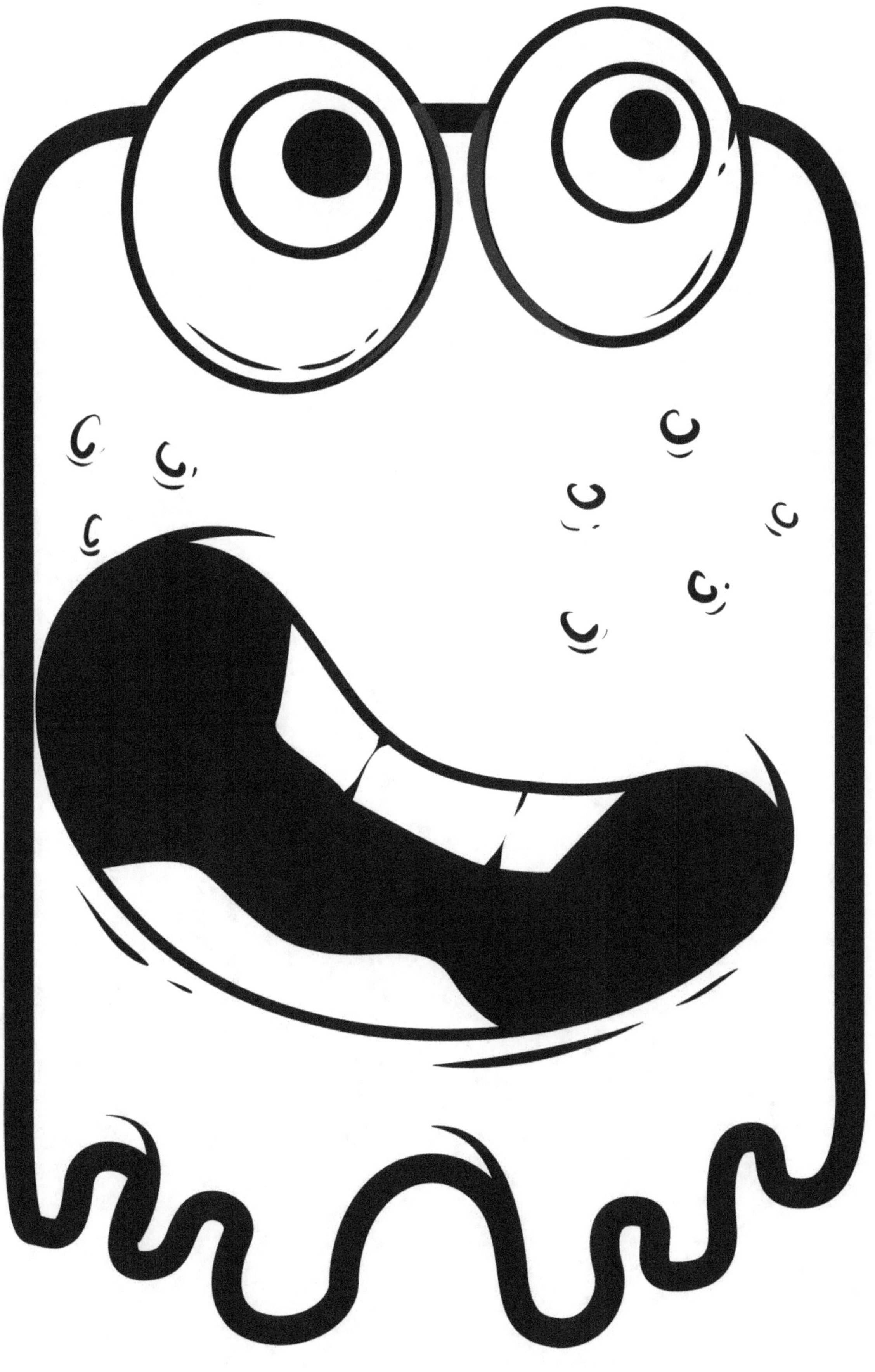

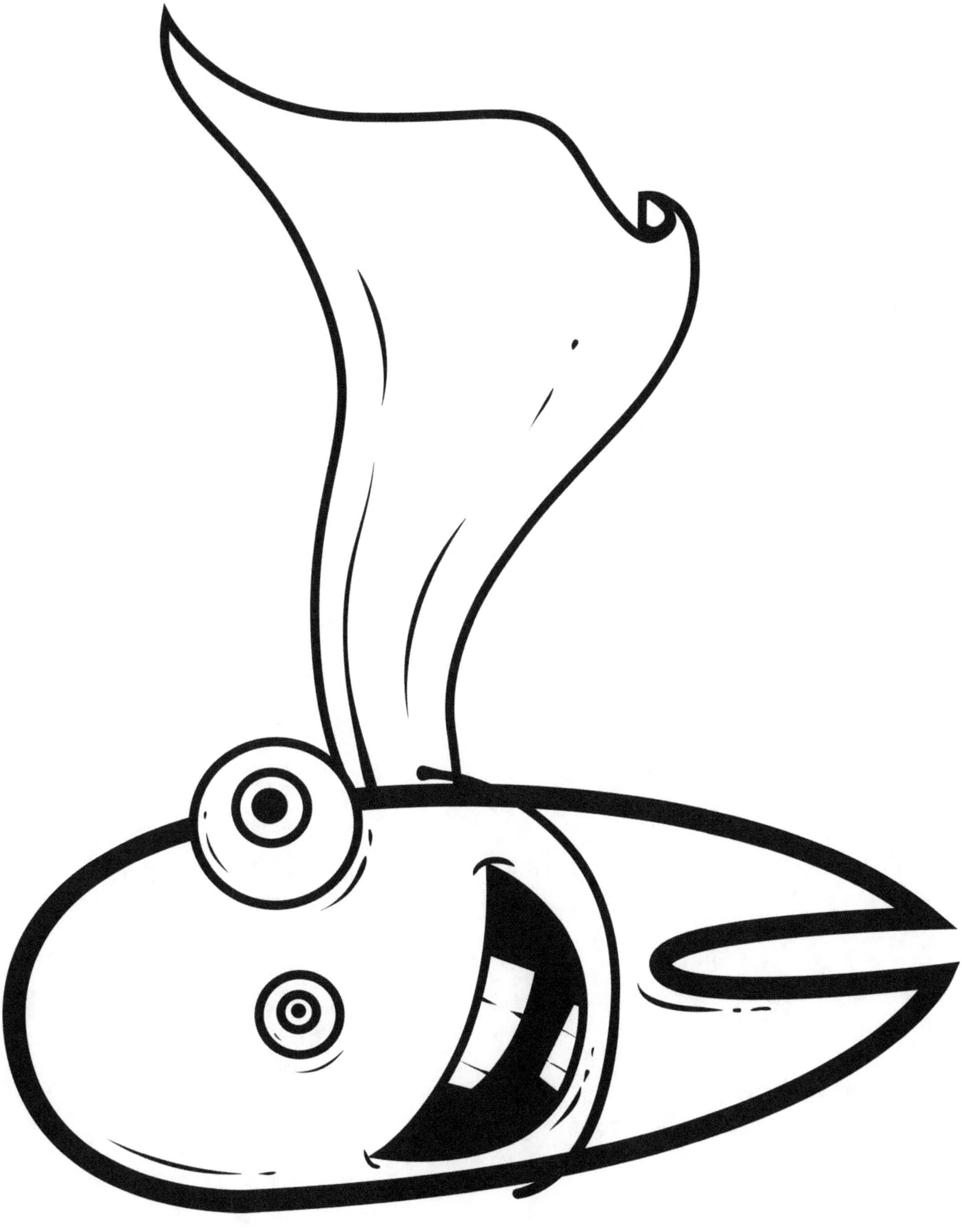

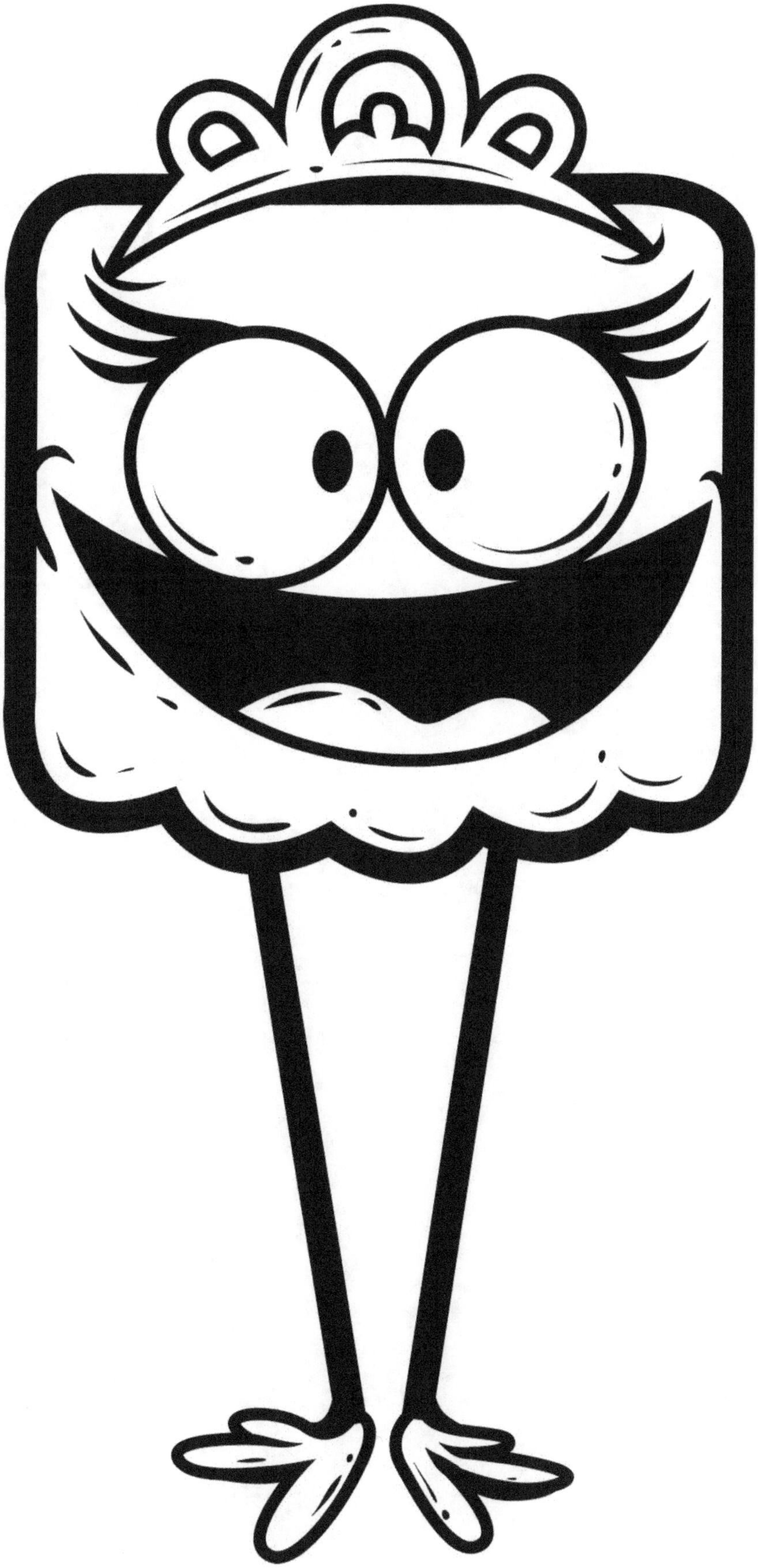

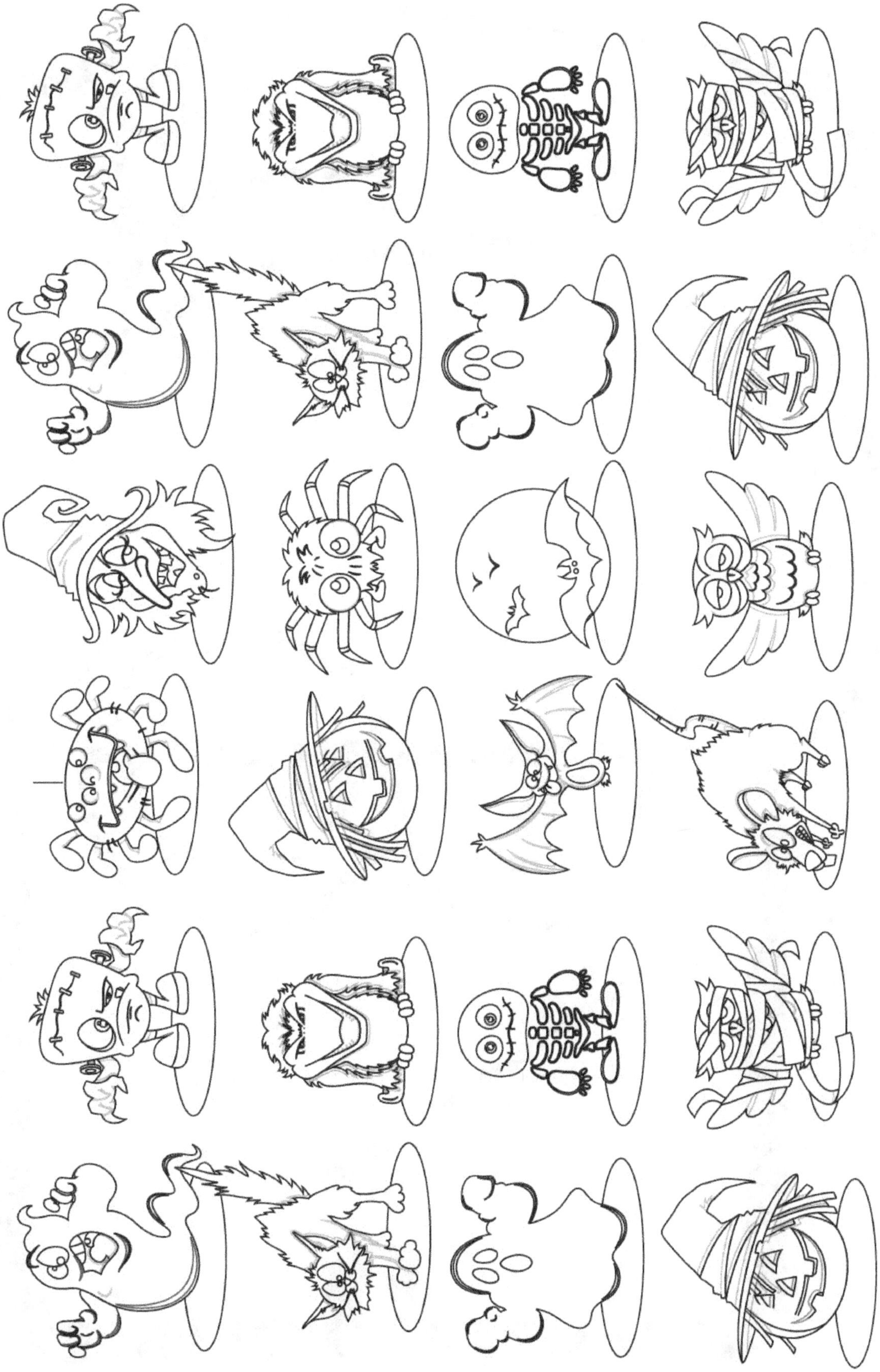

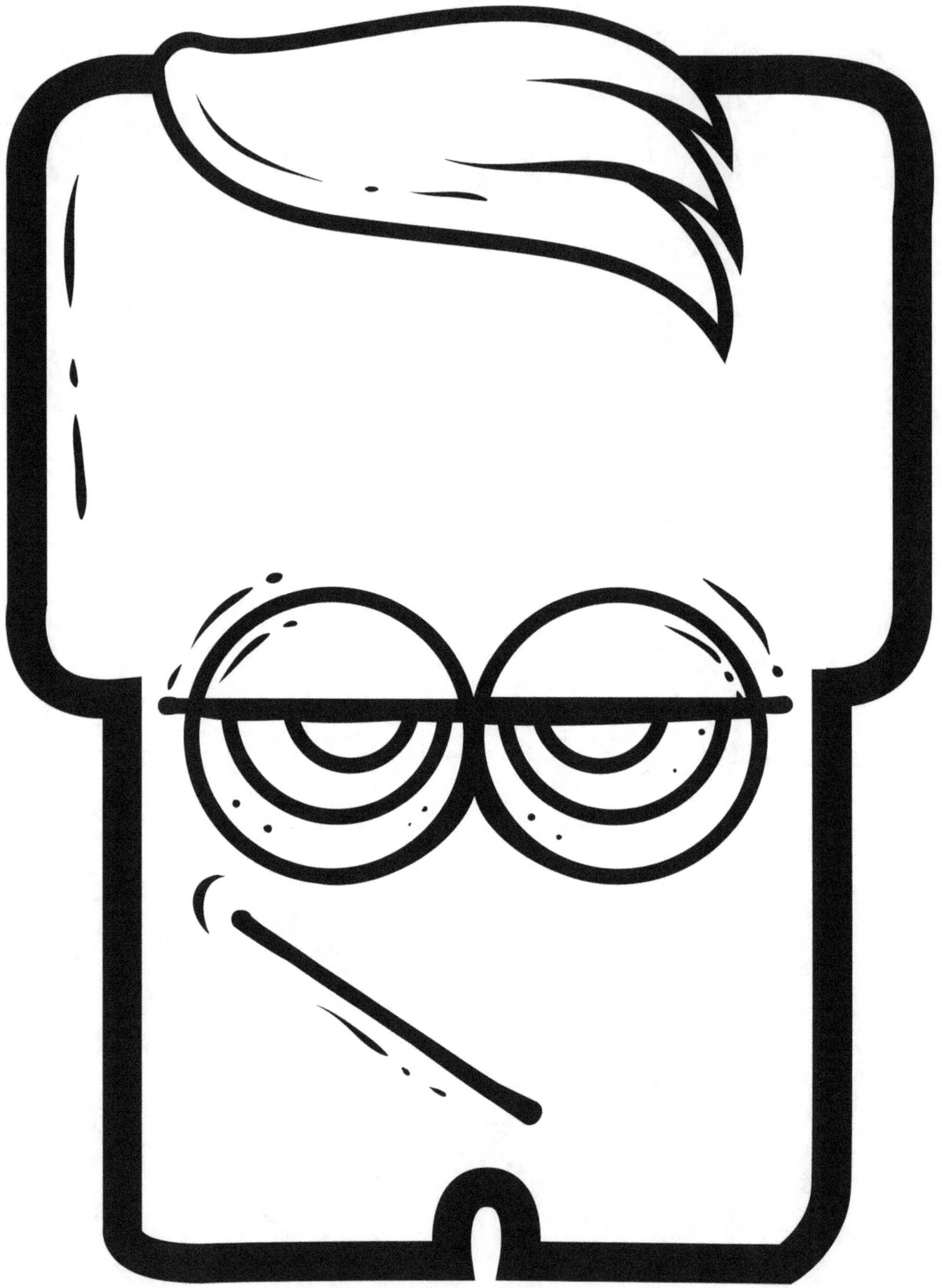

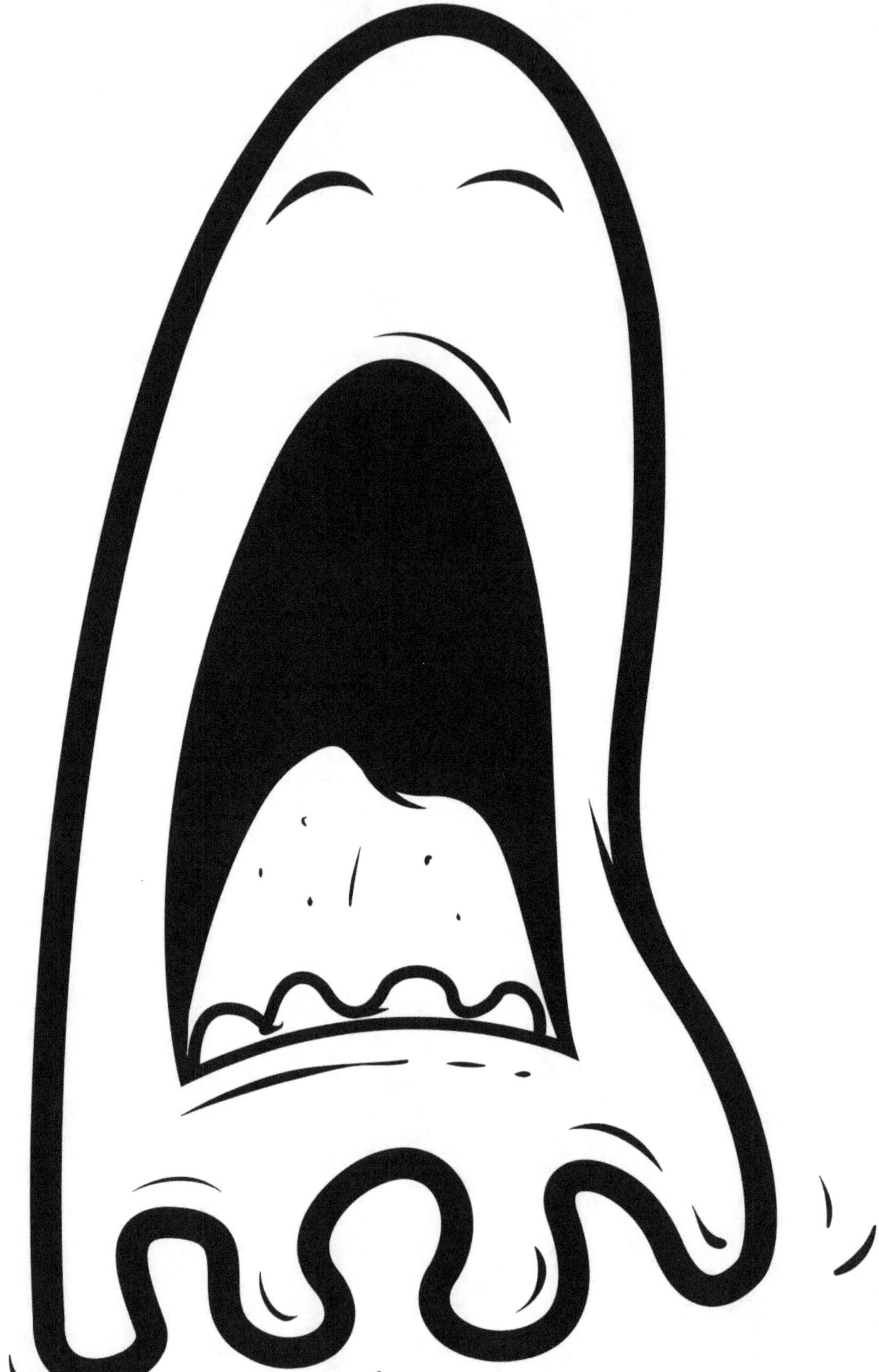

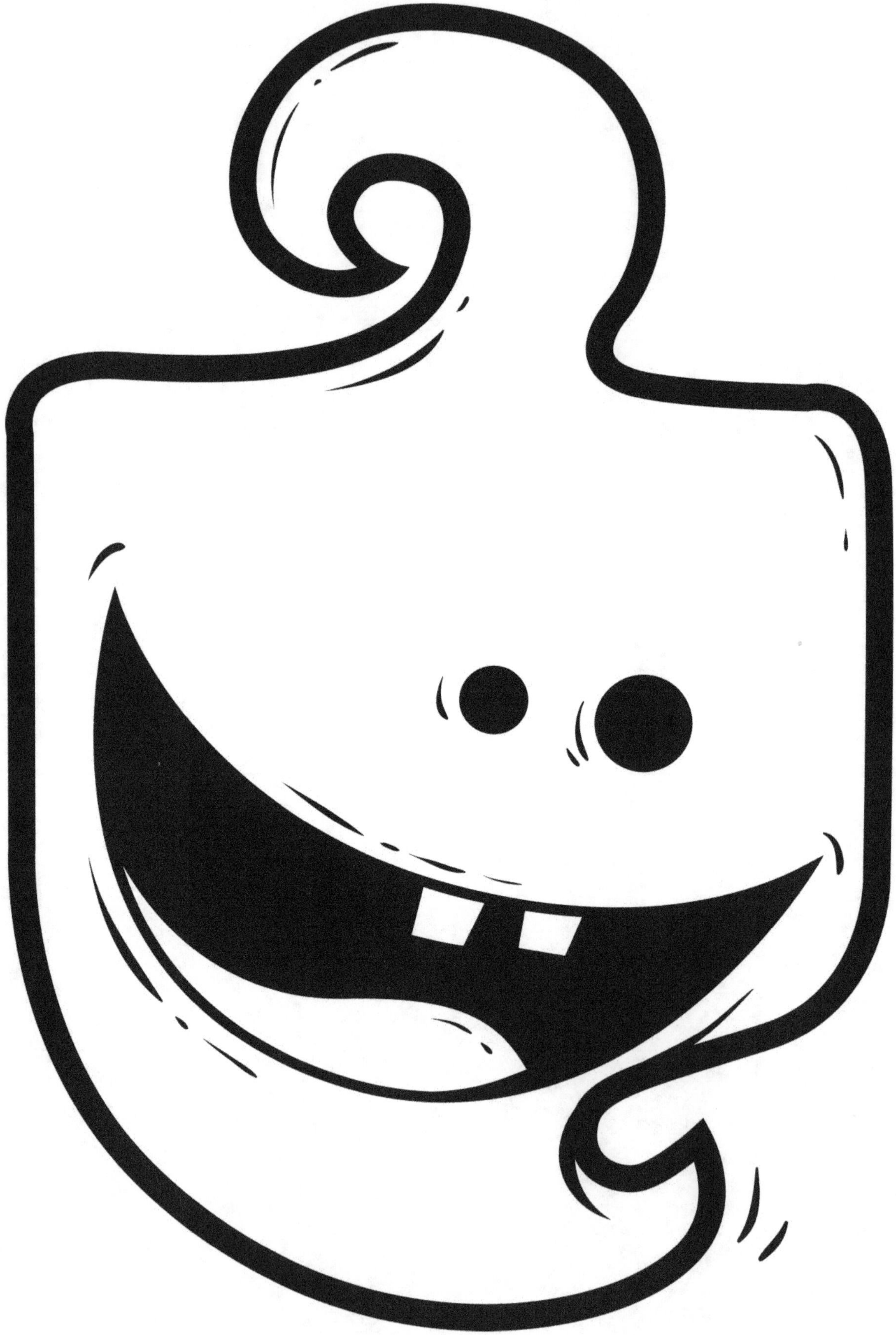

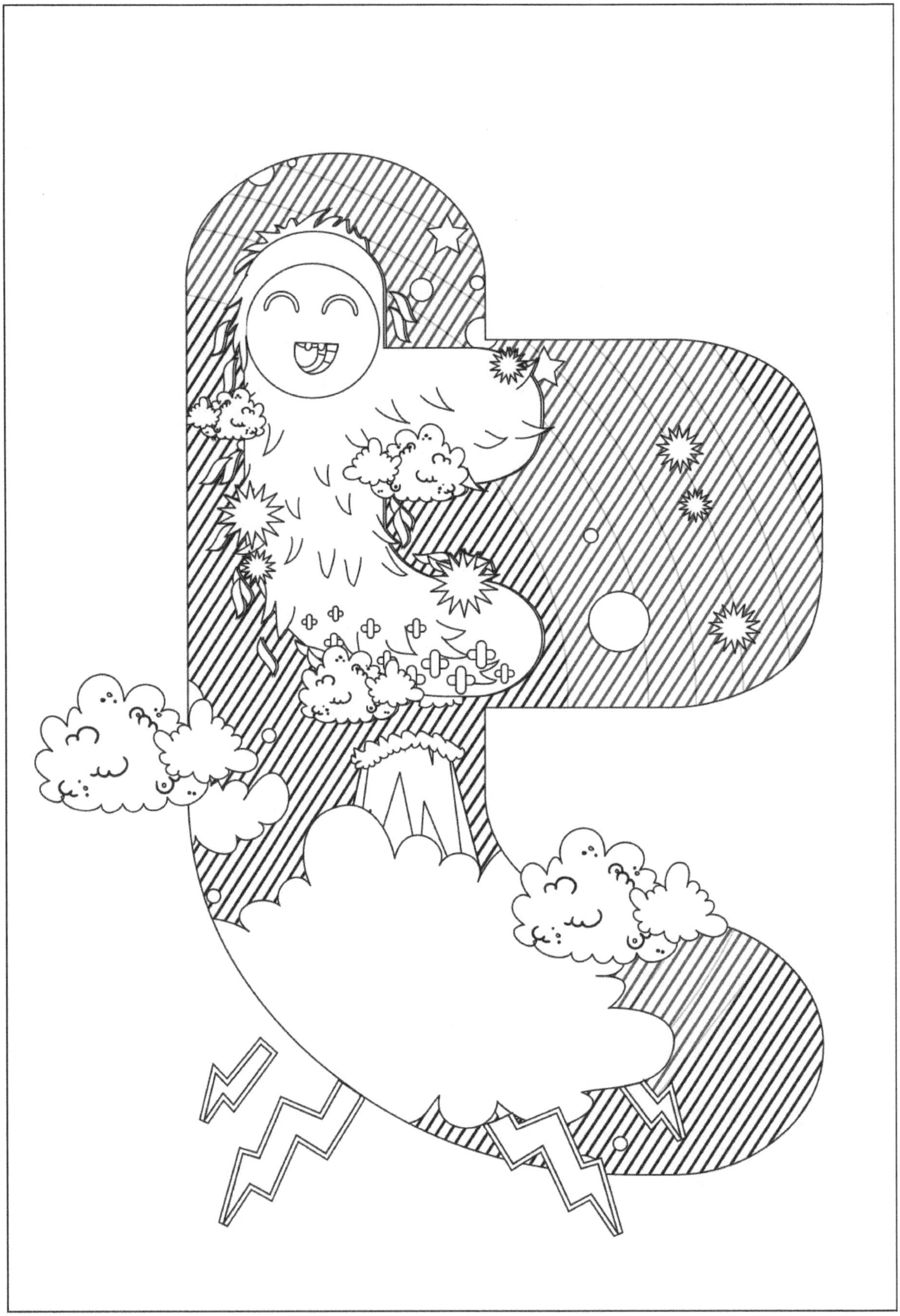

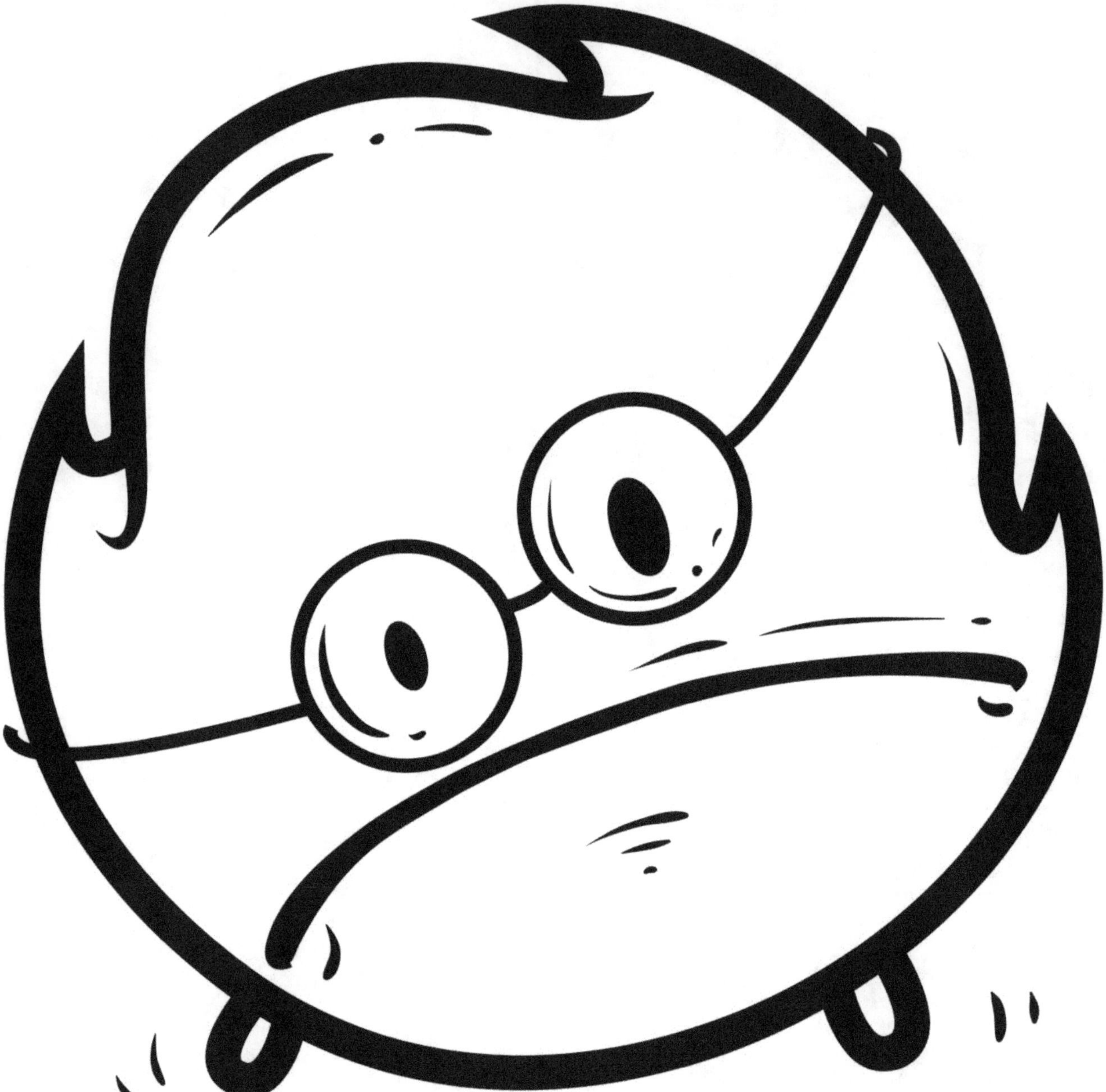

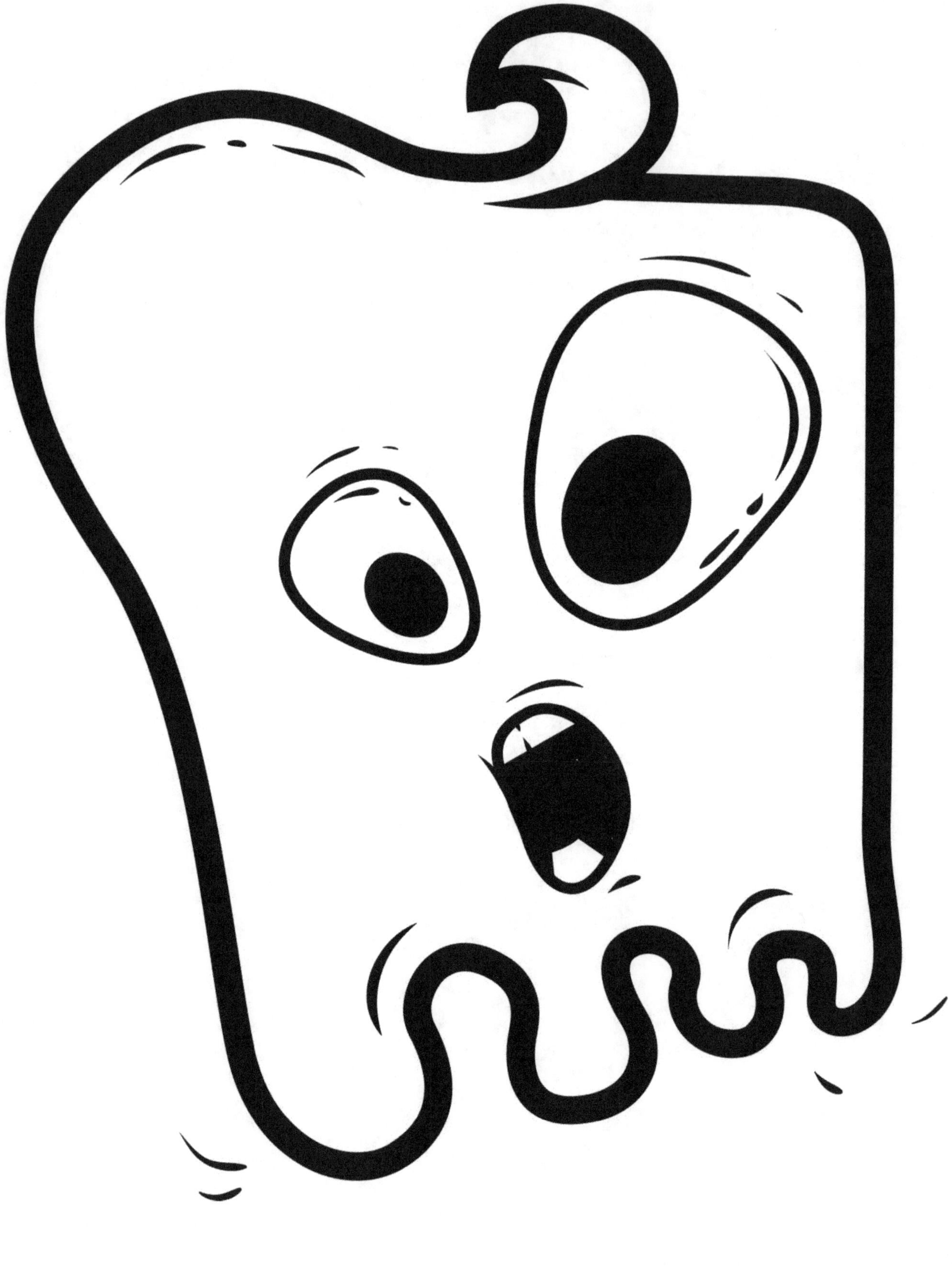

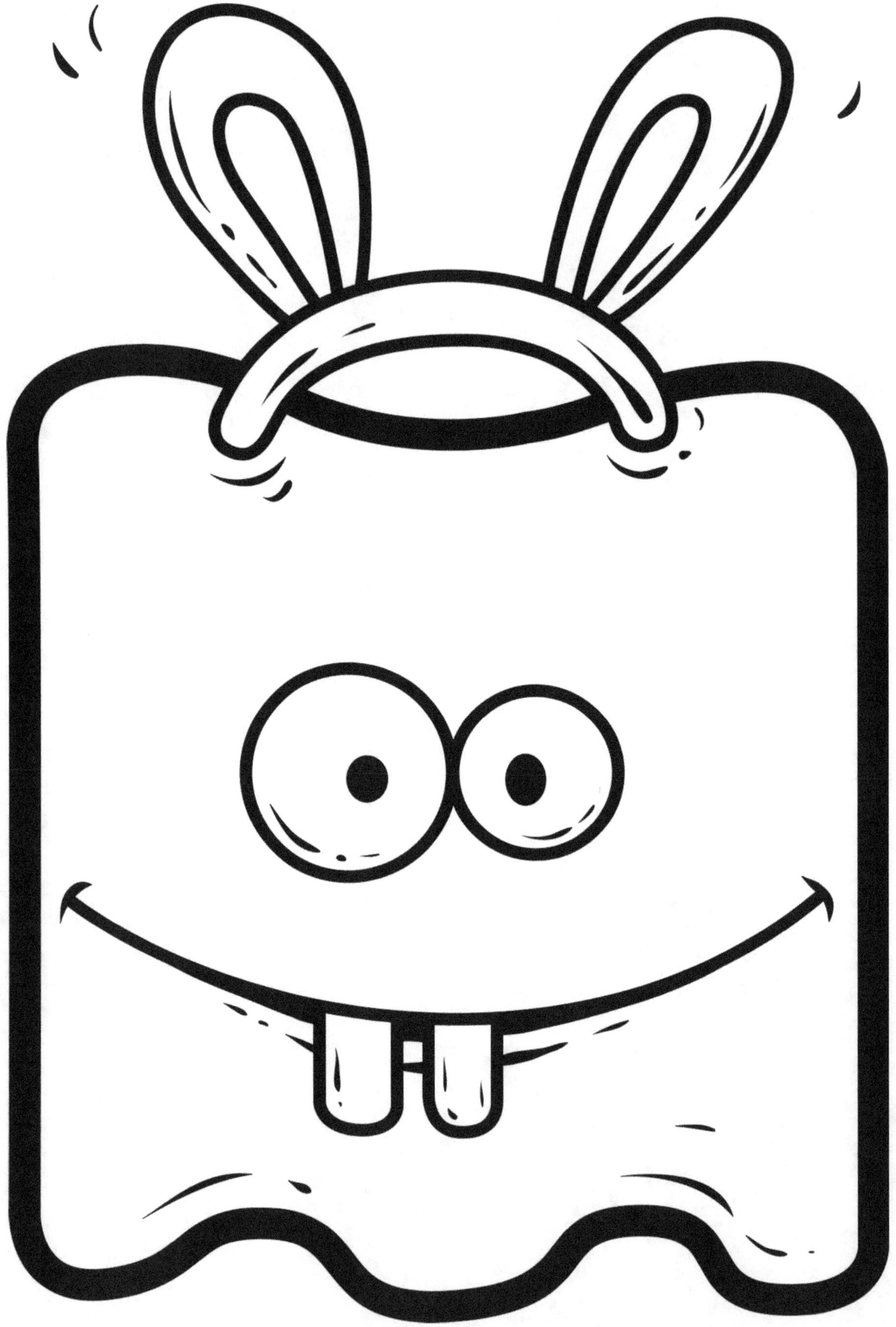

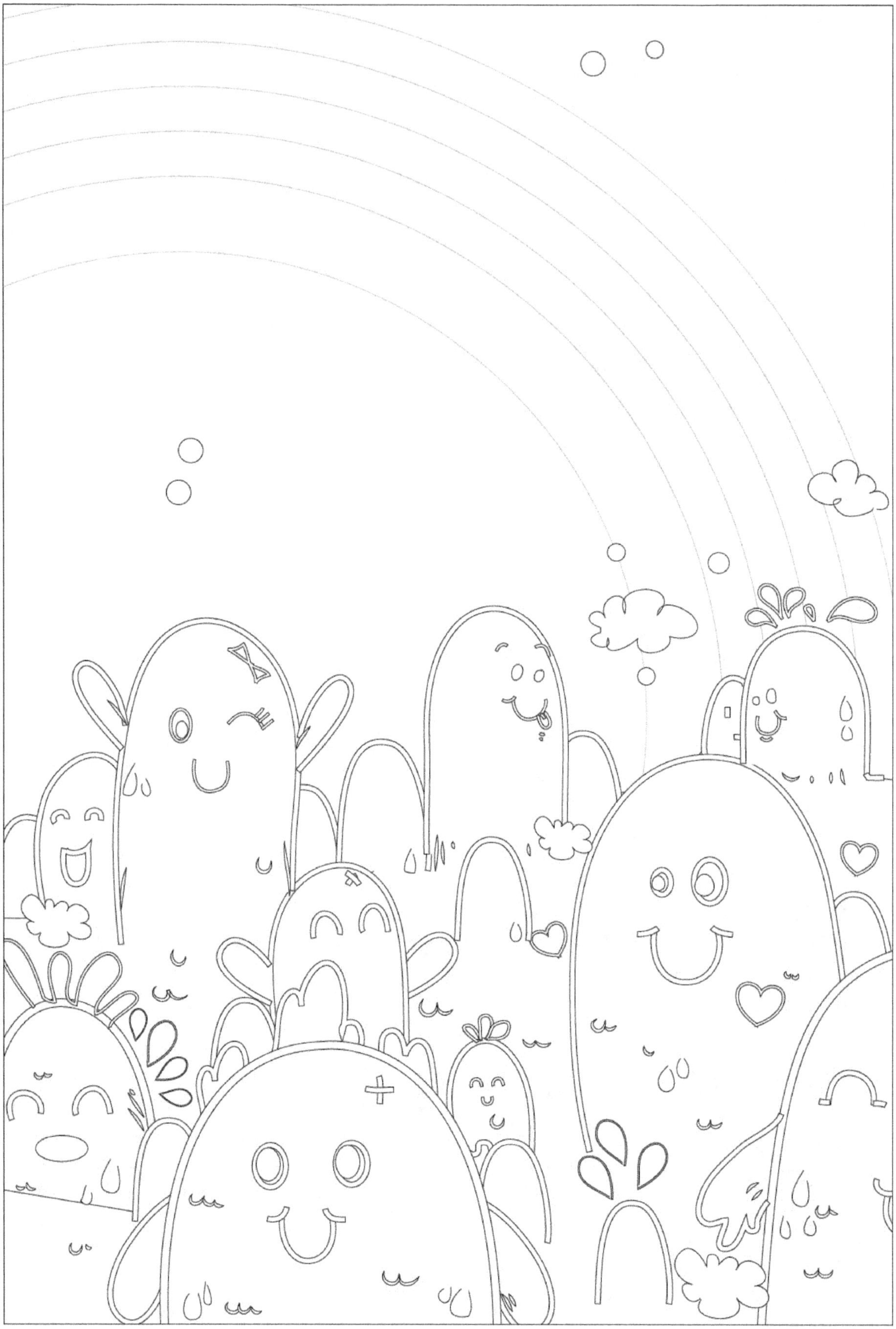

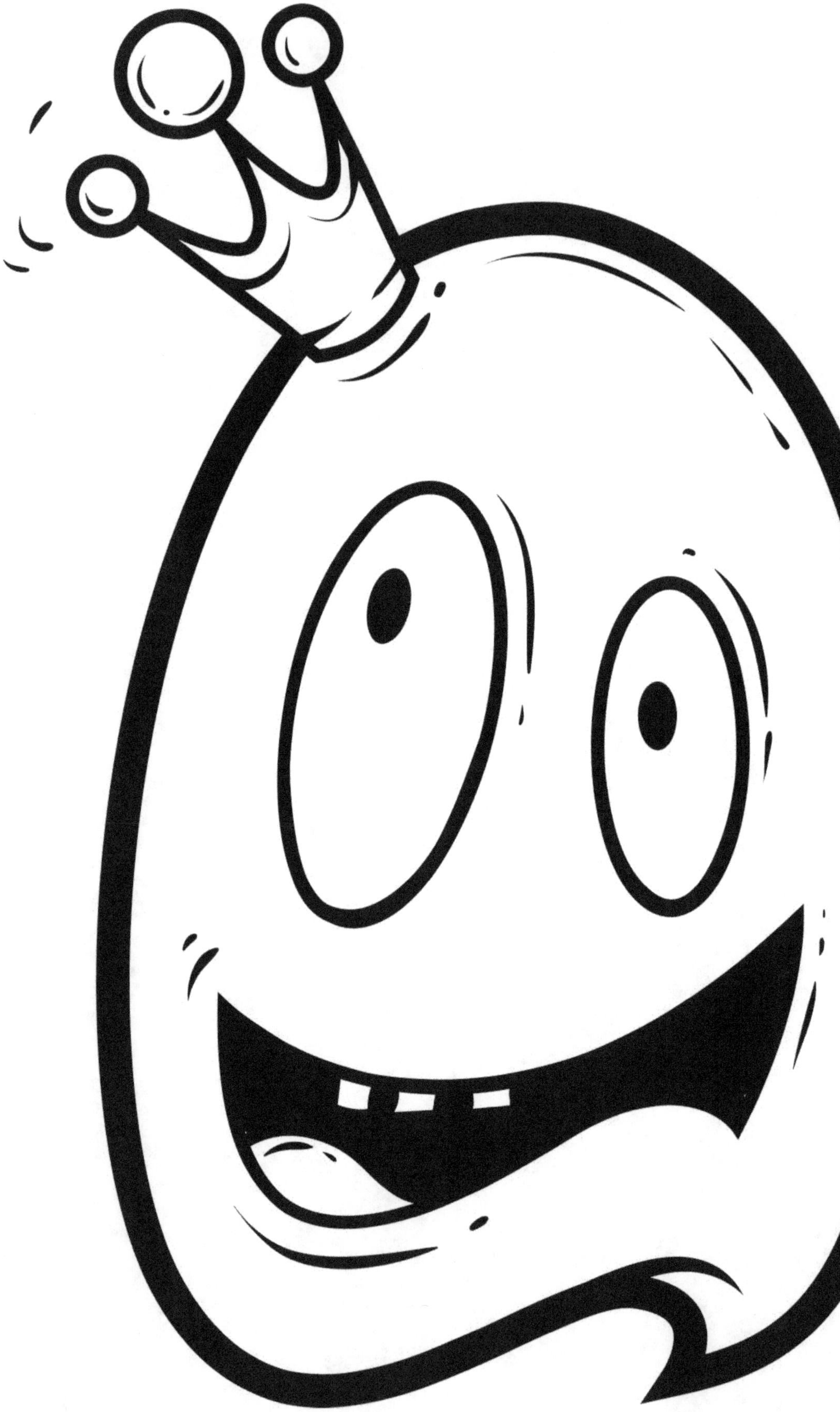

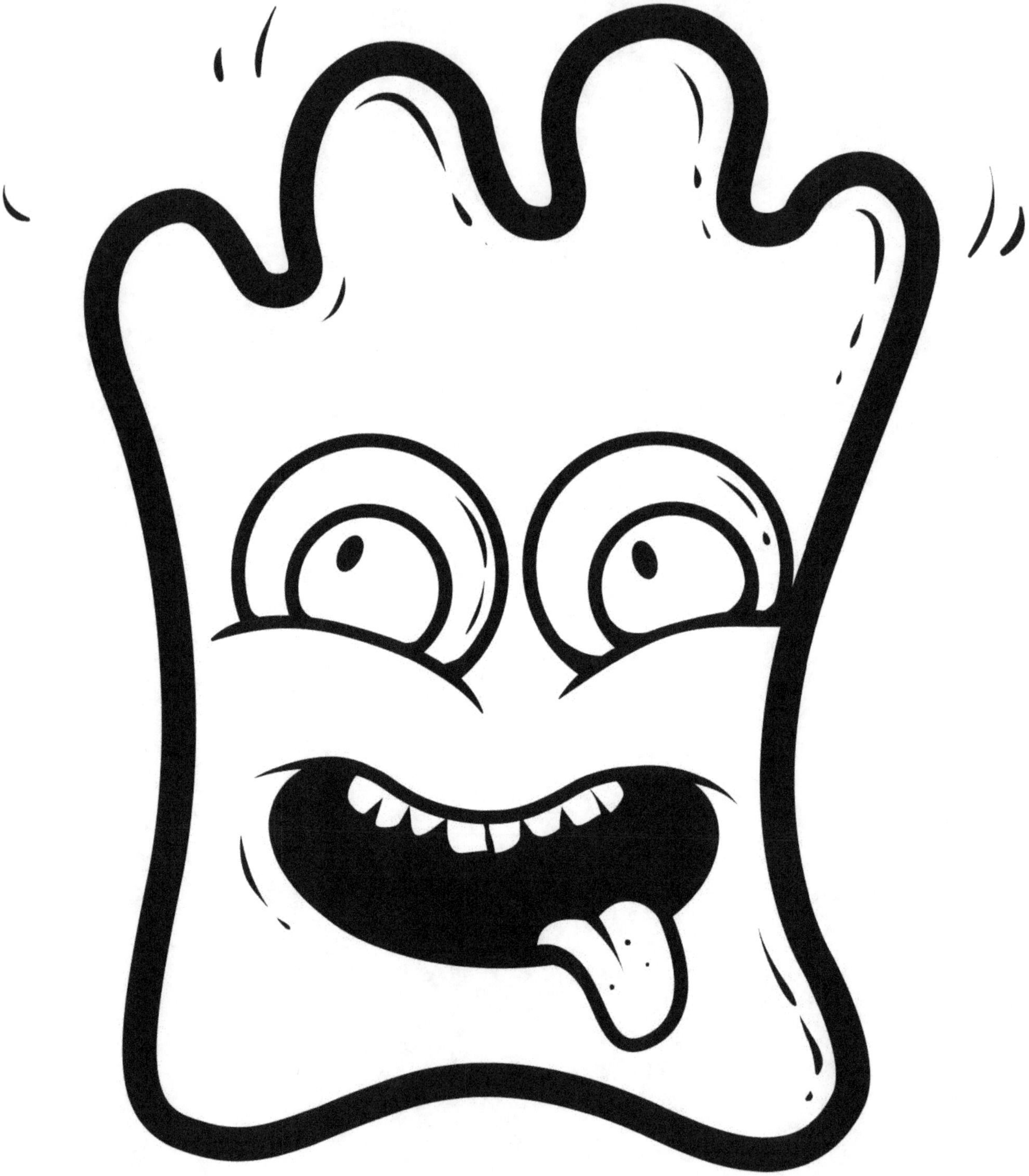

www.ingramcontent.com/pod-product-compliance
Lightning Source LLC
Chambersburg PA
CBHW080551190526
45169CB00007B/2722
* 9 7 8 1 5 3 5 2 3 1 4 5 9 *